For Alan Kay, my Dad and a
proud Geordie.

Tyne
Bridge
Publishing

GEORDIE NEWCASTLE
How we used to live

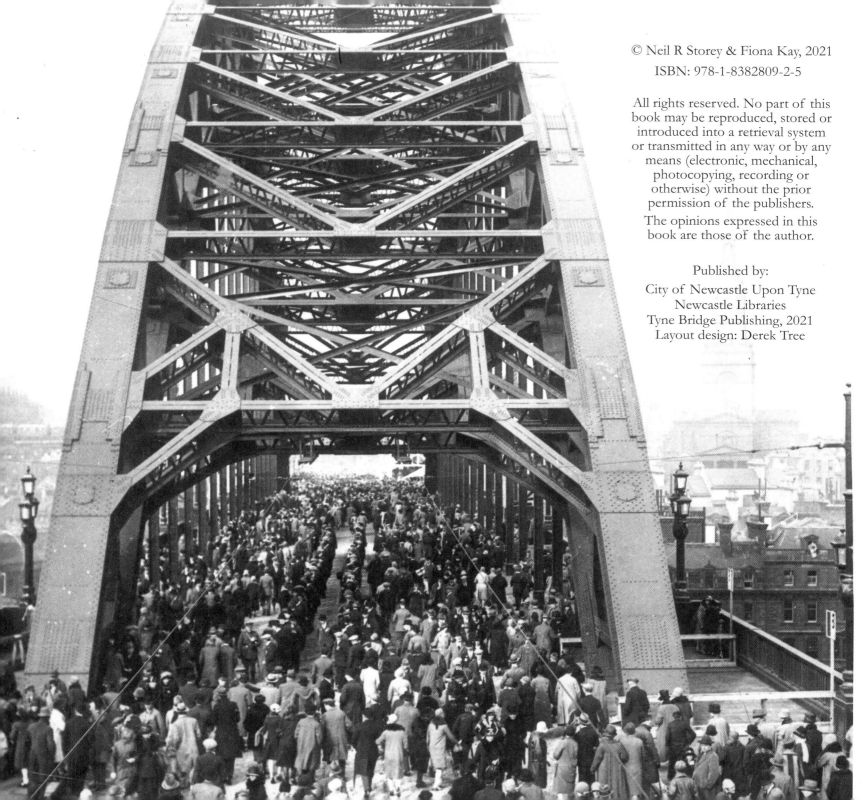

Published by:
City of Newcastle Upon Tyne
Newcastle Libraries
Tyne Bridge Publishing, 2021
Layout design: Derek Tree

CONTENTS

A dad and his children looking at the Quayside and city across the Tyne in the 1930s.
Such days out and the views of Newcastle are the stuff of memories.

Introduction

Many of us fortunate to be born and raised in old villages, towns and cities are born historians without realising it because, as we grow up, family and friends share their stories of the place and local people in the past. This is especially true of Geordie folk who grow up with an innate sense of local pride and identity entwined with a unique blend of dialect, wit, local culture, songs and sayings.

For some, very sadly, history is a subject that they lose an interest in at school. This is often because it is taught in a way that does not engage them, especially if its just a long stream of Kings and Queens and dates, no social history, no sense of place or empathy with those involved. Consequently there is very little the student can relate to or that holds their interest, it can seem irrelevant and they can end up disregarding history as a subject.

But time is a great healer and as we get a few years under our belts many people rekindle an interest in the past through nostalgia for their own memories and wishing they had paid more attention to the stories their parents and grandparents had told them, or had asked them about what they remembered of a particular place, event, or occasion in the past.

If you were born in the last half of the Twentieth Century, that's probably the majority of people who will be buying this book, our parents and grandparents lived through some of the greatest events and advances in British history. Some of them will have lived through the reigns of six different monarchs, two World Wars and knew a time where the horse was the driving force on the roads, before powered flight, talking films, colour films or even being able to listen to the radio or watch television.

This is a book of memories, it does not pretend to be encyclopaedic but it is a nostalgic look back at the Newcastle known to Geordie parents and grandparents and shows some of the places, shops, businesses and events they would have known. So, if you have heard of or can recall the likes of: Angus Watson 'The Sardine King,' Carrick's restaurants and bakers, Bainbridges department stores, Hadrian grocery shops or the Paramount Cinema; if you have ridden on the mat down the helter skelter at the Hoppings or if you can remember when trams and buses were emblazoned with the legend 'Shop at Binns,' the Quayside still had its cranes, the Tyne had big working shipyards, when a blue star shone over the Toon skyline and the city's buildings and monuments were blackened by soot, this is the book for you!

Neil R. Storey & Fiona Kay
2021

view of Grey Street opposite the Central Exchange Hotel in the 1930s.

"CANNY NEWCASTLE---The Pride o' the North."

'Canny Newcastle - The Pride o' the North' comic postcard c1905. The rain, smoke, grime and industry may be exaggerated but they were all things that were very much part and parcel of Newcastle at the time.

Newcastle viewed across the Tyne from The Rabbit Banks, Gateshead, c1890. In those days the river was lined with working factories, wharves and warehouses and the industries caused smog to hang in the air over the city.

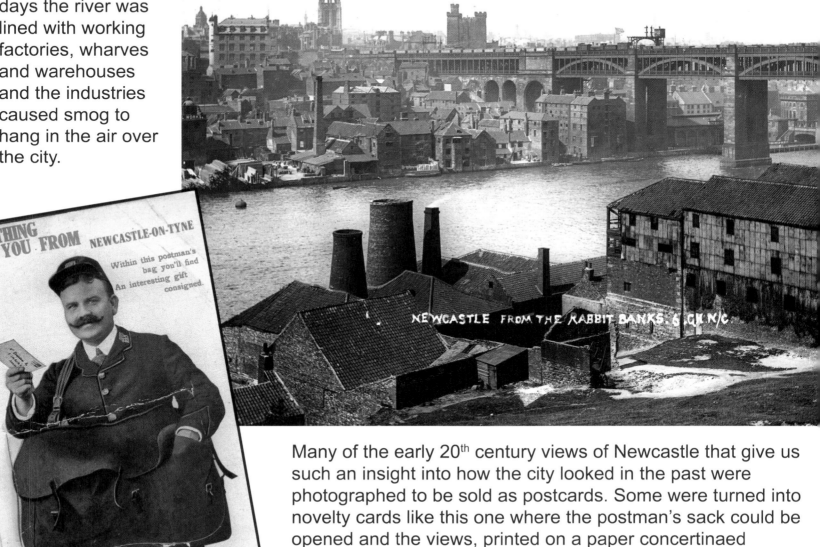

SOMETHING FOR YOU FROM NEWCASTLE-ON-TYNE

Within this postman's bag you'll find An interesting gift consigned.

NEWCASTLE FROM THE RABBIT BANKS. 6.GH N/C

834

Regd. No. 569 368

Many of the early 20th century views of Newcastle that give us such an insight into how the city looked in the past were photographed to be sold as postcards. Some were turned into novelty cards like this one where the postman's sack could be opened and the views, printed on a paper concertinaed behind, could be pulled out to be seen.

Chapter One

HOME IS WHERE THE HEART IS

The 1920s and 1930s were a time when there was a new fad for aerial photography, so let us begin with some wonderful aerial views of Newcastle in 1932. This view shows the Tyne Bridge, Quayside and gives us a great view of the railway bridge through the city.

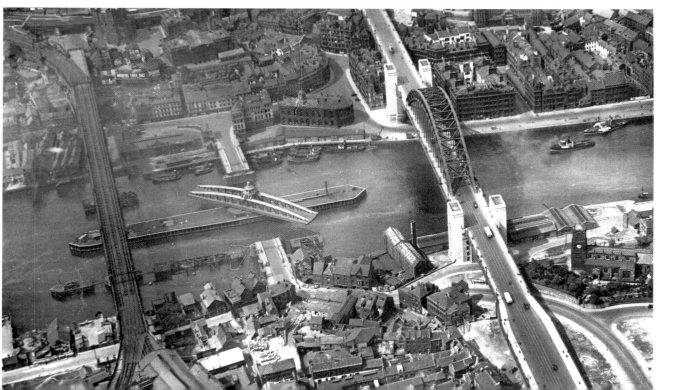

Its always good to see the Swing Bridge in operation and this aerial view captures the working Quaysides of both Newcastle and Gateshead in 1932.

The bustling city centre of Newcastle in 1932 viewed from Grey Street with Grey's Monument in the centre. In the upper left quarter we also get a lovely view of Old Eldon Square when the war memorial was surrounded by smart greens and trees.

Barras Bridge, the Church of St Thomas the Martyr (right) and the South African War Memorial in the triangle in the centre. Pictured in 1932, decades before the redevelopment that created the bus station, the area was always a hub for buses and trams.

Whitfield Road, Scotswood c1900. As the fortunes of the city and its people grew throughout the 19th century, the better off sought to buy or rent one of the thousands of new-build terraced houses that were spreading out from the city.

Tenements near Fenham Barracks c1890. Groups of women sat on doorsteps chatting, knitting, and carrying babies so they could 'get some fresh air' were seen on every street. Some folk even let their chickens out from their back yard coops to have a peck around the cobbles.

CHERRYBURN GARDENS, FENHAM.

WAITING FOR SOUP, S.ANN'S SOUP KITCHEN. NEWCASTLE. C1

Castle Garth with Dog Leap Stairs c1890. Although there was a certain Dickensian charm about it, the living conditions within these old buildings were often squalid and unsanitary and many folks simply did not have the money to move out from them.

"WASHING DAY" 1656.

Washing Day c1900 style. In those days a particular day of the week would be 'wash day' and women would gather with their washing dollies and tubs to get the task done. With no piped water to their houses, women would draw the water from communal taps or pumps they shared with their neighbours. A running joke was 'if the tap at the end of the raa' could talk it would have some stories to tell!

Left: Newcastle Corporation street cleaners and their 'dust cart' c1895. In the days when the horse was the driving force on the roads of Newcastle, the street cleaners were certainly kept busy.

Above: One of the Newcastle Corporation water carts fitted with a spray bar that would clop along the streets to help lay the dust, usually followed by the 'brush and flush' workmen who kept the streets clean and swept out the gutters c1895.

The frontages of 23-39 Ropery Walk, Pottery Bank, Walker, c1935. It is only the name and fading memories of old Pottery Bank that remain today.

The rears of Nos 17-5 Heworth View, Pottery Bank, Walker c1935. Victorian terraces and tenements were often hastily built to very poor standards. They were frequently prone to damp, relied on coal fires for heating and cooking and, despite many taking pride in what homes they could afford, these areas became worn, tired and difficult to maintain.

Times may have been hard but folks still liked to have a laugh together, including their pets. This Geordie family bought a second hand camera and backdrops and set up a studio in their garden in the 1920s. See if you can spot who has borrowed their mam's and sister's coats and hats.

A Newcastle family pose for the camera c1935. Life was tough for many working folk, even harder if the work dried up, especially for those with large families, some of ten or more children. Extended families, mam, dad, kids, grandma and grandad, often lived together in just a few rooms to make ends meet. Right: This Geordie mam has certainly got her hands full c1935.

A Salvation Army band c1939, once a familiar sight and sound on the terraced streets of Newcastle

Newcastle children c1940. Clothes were frequently home made, knitted or hand-me-downs which would be repaired if damaged, not thrown away. Children were also encouraged to polish their shoes before they went out. It was a matter of pride, no matter what their circumstances, most parents tried very hard to make sure their children were 'presentable'.

Children at one of a number of children's homes that were once in Newcastle c1942. They are well clothed, have toys and books provided charitably by many kind folks. Some of these children had been evacuated from London having lost one or both of their parents due to air raids.

Some of the boys outside The Newcastle Poor Children's Holiday Association & Rescue Agency Frances Nicholson Memorial Home and Orphanage, c1943.

The North is very much the home of the building society and by the 1930s more people than ever were able to save up for a deposit and obtain mortgages to buy their own home on one of the new housing estates, like this bungalow available from Wilkinson's for £425 in 1936.

In the 1930s a popular advertising gimmick were recipe booklets that could be obtained from various companies offering them in promotions whereby a mam would collect the specified number of wrappers and send them off and receive the booklet in return.

Mrs Mitchell in her pantry 1956. This lady was the mother of the family used to advertise the products on offer from Laws Stores, one of the first self-service supermarket chains in the North East.

Mrs Mitchell offers a treat of shortbread to her children in the ideal Geordie home lounge, complete with a photograph of King George VI greeting the Newcastle players over the mantelpiece, 1956. How many of your Mams had a pair of fluffy slippers like Mrs Mitchell?

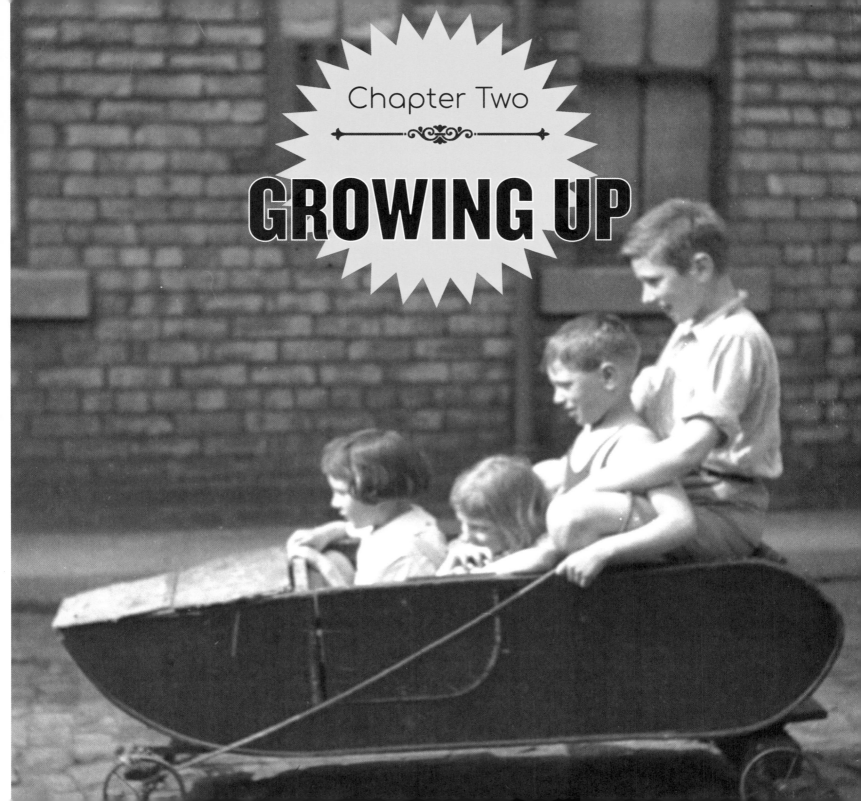

Chapter Two

GROWING UP

Children playing in the street and gutter on Westmorland Road, Elswick. Behind them is a horse-drawn milk cart and the Villa Victoria pub c1900.

Newcastle schoolgirls practising their left handed salute for the parade in honour of the Coronation of King George V in 1911. Right, advert for Wilkin's Cremona Toffee Royal Family Assortment, a treat for all the family, made at the Cremona Park Factory for the Coronation of George VI in 1937.

The World's Garden Toffery.

20 different kinds

Toffee, Nougat, Fresh Cream Caramels

Think of all the good things used in making good Toffee. Add to them Rich thick Cream. Think, then, of spotless gleaming Model Kitchens, and set them in the crisp, clean, fresh Air of the Northumberland Countryside: NOW you have the background for

Wilkin's

CREMONA

"ROYAL"

'Family' Assortment

made only by WILKIN at Cremona Park, for all who love GOOD TOF

Some of the lads of The Life Boys, the junior reserve of The Boys' Brigade, proudly showing off the Temperley Cup they won at the St Barnabas Pageant, Newcastle c1930.

Children of St Jude's Sunday School, Shieldfield, c1942.

Heaton Congregational Church Girl Guides, January 1945.

Byker Boys'
Brigade
outside of
Byker Parish
Hall,
September
1945.

The St Francis Church Girls' Brigade, October 1942.

Prize winning team from St Paul's Scout Troop, Elswick, proudly wearing their many proficiency badges in 1940.

Many girls dreamed of being a ballerina and a number of schools of ballet and dance existed in Newcastle. Dating from March 1944, this group's performances undoubtedly brought a ray of sunshine to wartime audiences.

Officers and drums of the Newcastle Sea Cadet Corps, June 1946.

Girls Training Corps on parade at Whickham View School, July 1944.

The choir of the Parish Church of St Michael, Byker, June 1944. With strong Church of England, Catholic and non-conformist communities in and around Newcastle many youngsters were members of their local church choir.

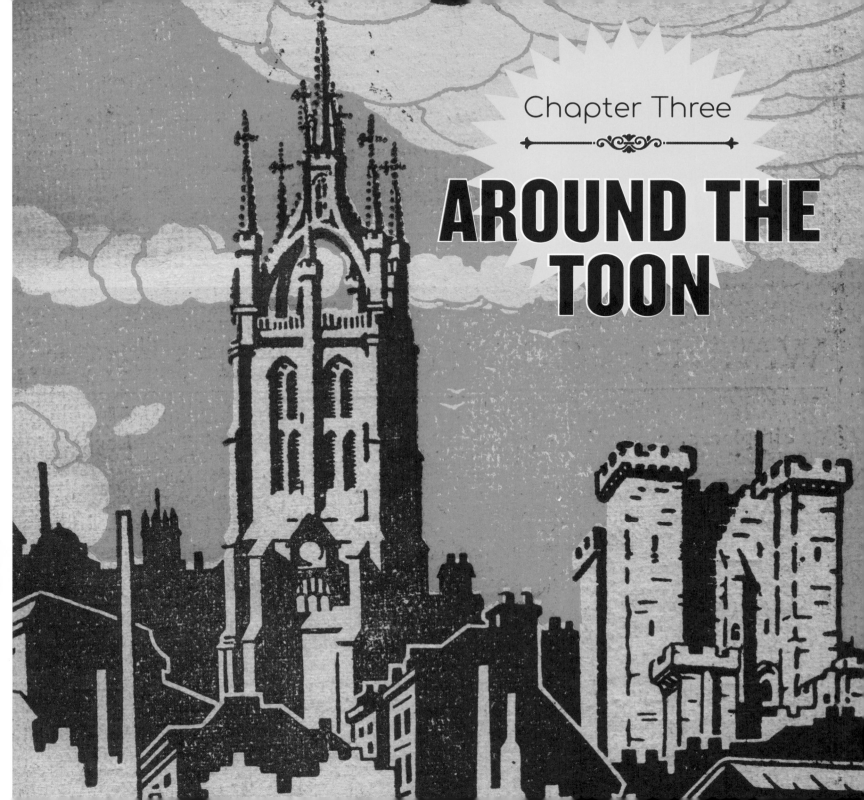

Chapter Three

AROUND THE TOON

THE SILVER JUBILEE

BRITAIN'S FIRST STREAMLINE TRAIN

NEWCASTLE AND LONDON IN 4 HOURS

AVERAGE THROUGHOUT SPEED 67·08 M.P.H.
Weekdays from 30th. September 1935
NEWCASTLE dep 10·0 | KING'S CROSS dep 5·30
DARLINGTON — 10·42 | DARLINGTON arr 8·48
KING'S CROSS arr 2·0 | NEWCASTLE arr 9·30

Inclusive Fares First Class 5/- Third Class 3/7.

LONDON & NORTH EASTERN RAILWAY

Newcastle Central Station with waiting cabs and trams passing outside c1910. Note the boy on the far right has bare feet. Shoes were a luxury for the children of some families and if they did have footwear it would be reserved for school days and attending church. Left: Frank Newbould's poster for the Silver Jubilee train which travelled between London and Newcastle from 1935 and was named in honour of George

The first view many have of Newcastle upon leaving Central station and heading towards the city centre up Grainger Street, pictured on a rainy day c1910.

Below: A Kodak Limited paper wallet from their Granger Street shop c1935, from the days when most people took their photographic films to shops for developing and printing.

Grainger Street, c1930. On the left just beyond H. Samuel's jewellers can be seen the long frontage and tall gold lettering of Isaac Walton & Co Tailors and Outfitters, where many Newcastle school children were fitted for their school uniforms.

GRAINGER STREET & GREYS MONUMENT, NEWCASTLE-ON-TYNE.   G.8400.

Grainger Street c1938 with John Moses department store on the left spanning the corner of Nelson Street and extending up Grainger Street.

Clayton Street c1900

The Grainger Market with its wonderful array of shops and stalls c1925, even today it remains one of the largest market halls in the world. Inset: An earlier colour image of the market.

Grey's Monument 1947. The YMCA building to the left on the corner of Blackett Street was used during the war by the military. Post war the signs state 'Now being re-conditioned for civilian membership.' The building was pulled down to make way for Eldon Square shopping centre. Directly behind the Monument is the Post Office.

Blackett Street, c1900. There were trams, bicycles and even a few motor cars but when this photograph was taken the horse still ruled the roads.

Eldon Square and war memorial c1933, when it was still surrounded by Georgian houses, an area of tranquil calm in the city centre.

A busy St Andrew's Street filled with lorries of fresh fruit and vegetables delivering to The Green Market (on the left), 1959

Westgate Road, c1955, when this area offered shops, cafes and entertainments from Woolf's department store to the 2,000-seater Essoldo cinema.

The junction of Blackett Street, Pilgrim Street (left) and Northumberland Street (right) viewed from New Bridge Street, c1920. The most distinctive feature missing from this view is Newcastle's very own golden girl statue and clock which were installed on the corner of the Northern Goldsmiths Company building in 1935.

Advert for Reid & Sons Goldsmiths and Jewellers of Blackett Street, 1919. This business has been a part of Newcastle life since 1778.

A bustling Northumberland Street decorated for the Silver Jubilee celebrations of King George V in 1935.

Fenwick

Northumberland St., Newcastle-on-Tyne

Northumberland Street, Newcastle. 8703

Northumberland Street c1925 which along with Grainger Street formed the shopping heartland of Newcastle. On the left is Fenwick's where our mams would go for something extra special from their French Salon, offering the latest fashion from gay Paris or wedding gifts from its beautiful glass and china department.

French Hat SHOW

Fenwick

Mr J. J. FENWICK'S FRENCH SALON.

THE TERRACE TEA ROOM,
FENWICK LTD.   NEWCASTLE-ON-TYNE

Fenwick's Terrace Tea room c1935 where luncheon and high tea were accompanied by genteel live music.

Woolworths was renowned for its fine displays like this whole area offering briar pipes at 6d a time in 1939. In the days before the dangers of smoking were widely promoted, any dapper 'man about town' who wished to affect an air of maturity and sophistication smoked a pipe.

One the of brand new developments within the Northumberland Street 'Woolies' in 1937 was the refreshment bar where workers and shoppers could pop in for a quick snack from a bill of fare that included ham rolls at 2d or fish cakes and chips or pie and mash all for 6d a time.

Lawsons chocolate shop, 1936. Proudly branded as 'Newcastle's Chocolate Makers', owner Jack Lawson had shops in the city and a confectionery works in Gosforth. Note the vending machine outside described in those days as 'The automatic shop that never shuts.'

The affectionately remembered F W Woolworth 3d and 6d goods store on Northumberland Street. Originally opened in 1913 it is seen here with its newly completed extension in 1937. Do you remember the milk bar or the pick 'n' mix?

Pilgrim Street in 1947 and, right, Nun Street in 1949.

Left: Grey Street c1925. When this photograph was taken Grey Street, another triumph of builder and developer Richard Grainger, was not 100 years old.

Bainbridge's 'Man's Shop' and Gentleman's Hairdressing saloon, Grainger Street 1936.

Bainbridge's store on Market Street c1910 claimed to the 'The Largest Store in the North'. This was one of three Bainbridge stores that were, in their day, part and parcel of a shopping trip to Newcastle. Inset: Advert for Bainbridge's department stores c1930.

The Bigg Market c1930. This area always seemed to be bustling with small crowds, not only visiting its shops or as visitors to events held at the old town hall but they were also drawn to the market stalls, notably Risi's and Mark Toney's ice creams.

The Bigg Market in 1947 with the Rutherford Fountain in the foreground.

St Nicholas Cathedral, c1900. Note the cabmen's shelter and horse-drawn hackney carriages in the foreground, there is neither a steam nor motor vehicle in sight.

Black Gate and Castle, St Nicholas Street, c1950.

Sandhill and The Side, c1895. In the foreground are the carriers' horses, carts and shelters but it was a stiff old climb for the hand barrow carters who transported goods from Quayside to Toon.

A bustling Quayside and the newly completed Tyne Bridge c1928.

The Tyne Bridge in the 1930s. Not just a symbol of Newcastle but the backdrop for thousands of memories and stories. Even now after all these years, rail passengers crane their heads in carriages to see the structure as they rattle over the railway bridge.

The Milk Bar, New Bridge Street, 1938. The promotion of public health and fitness during the 1930s saw the American idea of milk bars offering an array of tasty milkshakes instead of alcoholic beverages adopted in Britain.

A balloon and paper flower seller amongst the crowds at the Quayside Sunday Market c1933.

Thousands throng the Quayside for the Sunday Market c1929.

Sunday Market stall of parts and valves for radios c1933. In the days before television people would sit around their 'wireless' in their sitting rooms in much the same way, listening to the news, music, entertainment programmes and sporting commentaries. However, radios were expensive and folks kept theirs going with new vales and regular repairs.

Roll up folks and get your
Bon Bons - tuppence a bag
at the Sunday Market, 1933.

Quayside Sunday Market traders 'barking up' sales of their fresh fruit c1933.

Chapter Four

A JOB OF WORK

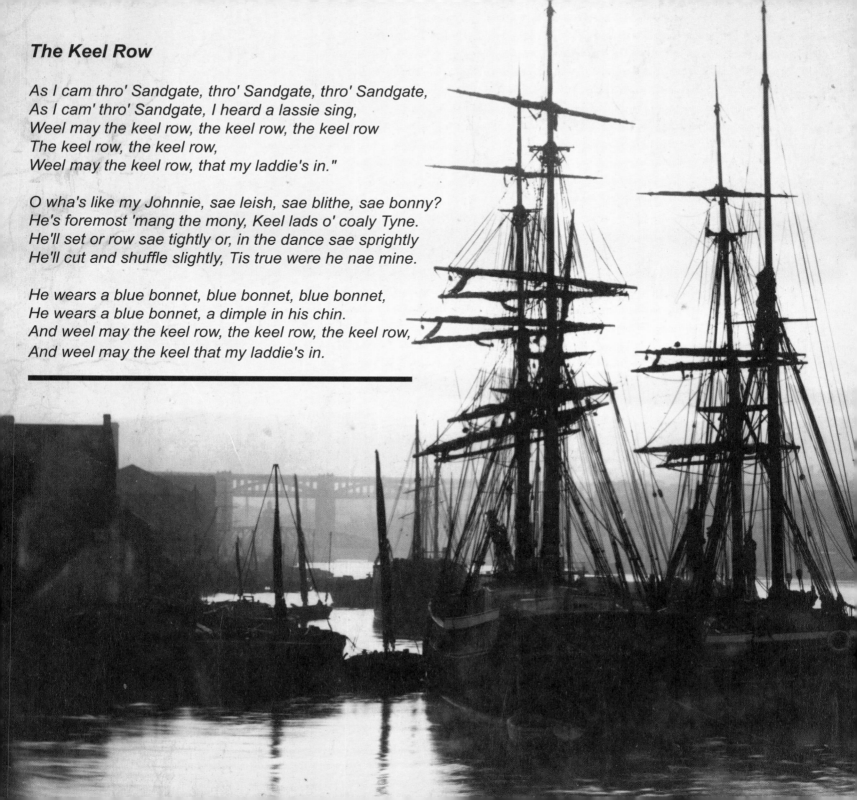

The Keel Row

As I cam thro' Sandgate, thro' Sandgate, thro' Sandgate,
As I cam' thro' Sandgate, I heard a lassie sing,
Weel may the keel row, the keel row, the keel row
The keel row, the keel row,
Weel may the keel row, that my laddie's in."

O wha's like my Johnnie, sae leish, sae blithe, sae bonny?
He's foremost 'mang the mony, Keel lads o' coaly Tyne.
He'll set or row sae tightly or, in the dance sae sprightly
He'll cut and shuffle slightly, Tis true were he nae mine.

He wears a blue bonnet, blue bonnet, blue bonnet,
He wears a blue bonnet, a dimple in his chin.
And weel may the keel row, the keel row, the keel row,
And weel may the keel that my laddie's in.

A plan of the River Tyne showing its shipyards, docks and quays 1904. All the traditional ship builders have gone, the marine engineers that have revived some of the industry use modern methods and today it is not possible to buy a single ship's rivet on the Tyne.

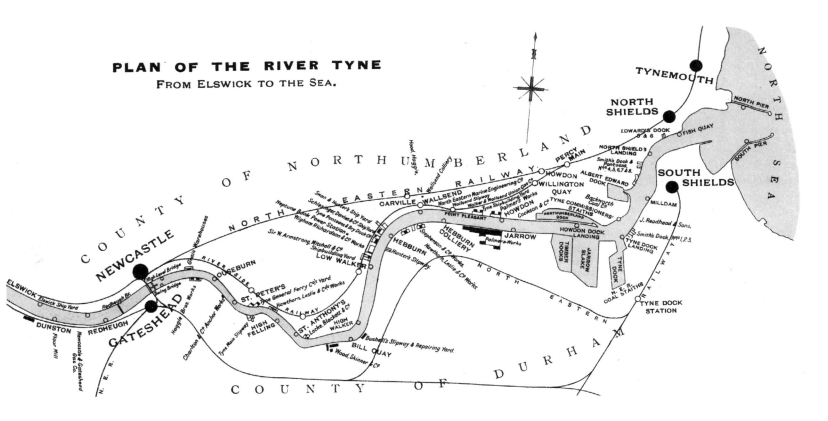

Outside the city walls was Sandgate, one of the poorest and most overcrowded areas of Newcastle where the redoubtable workers known as the keelmen lived. Their labours were to collect the coal for shipment in their keels from the chutes or 'spouts' along the Tyne and row them over to the waiting collier ships where they would then shovel it into the hold. The nineteenth century developments of coal staithes along the Tyne that enabled coal ships to be filled direct from the staithe and into steam boats saw the work of keelmen disappear, and this centuries old job of work was little more than a memory by the early 20th century. The memory of the keelmen is kept alive in the local folk song 'The Keel Row.' Like any folk song there are slightly different versions, see opposite page for one of the most popular.

Elswick Works c1900. Established by William George Armstrong in 1847. By the 1940s the works provided employment for thousands, extended to over a mile along the Tyne and covered 70 acres.

LAUNCH OF THE S.S. MAURETANIA.
THE LARGEST SHIP IN THE WORL
SEP.T. 20 1906
5250

Above: RMS *Mauretania* on the Tyne, 1906. In her day the 'Maury' was the largest ship, indeed the largest moving structure in the world. By 1909 she took both the east and west bound 'Blue Ribands' for fastest crossings of the Atlantic, an accolade she held for 20 years.

MARINE ENGINEERS

SHIPBUILDERS

SWAN HUNTER & WIGHAM RICHARDSON LIMITED

WALLSEND & NEWCASTLE UPON TYNE

Launch of the RMS *Mauretania* 20, September 1906, built by Wigham Richardson and Swan Hunter for Cunard. Within she had state rooms and accommodation that were both elegant and the height of fashion.

HMS Victoria passing through the Swing Bridge, 1889. It was a tradition for local people of all ages to watch newly completed ships steam out along the Tyne.

Men and women workers at the Wallsend Slipway Engineering Company during the First World War. Women took the place of men and helped to expand the workforce needed for the war effort in both world wars.

Approaching the Swing Bridge, photographed from a vessel on the Tyne 1958. To the right are the cranes that were once a familiar sight along the Tyne.

Unloading a cargo of timber onto the Quayside c1930.

Railway navvies and engineers pause from their work beside the huge railway crossing at the Central station c1895.

Wallsend Colliery, (later known as Rising Sun Colliery) shortly after it opened in 1910. For the generations that come after the closure of our mines it is hard to imagine the landscape around Newcastle, Northumberland and Durham punctuated by the pit wheels of hundreds of working collieries.

Miners walking home from the pit on Welbeck Road, Walker, June 1901. The sound of hundreds of heavy, leather soled working men's boots from pits and ship yards all knocking off at the same time was a sound that echoed across the streets of the industrial north.

Some of the lads from one of the local coal mines c1920. Many would have started work down the pits as young as 14.

Elswick Works Fire Brigade c1910. Many of the larger places of employment had their own fire brigades and every industrial place of work encouraged the training of staff in first aid to good degrees of proficiency. Annual competitions were held between first aid teams from various businesses and organisations.

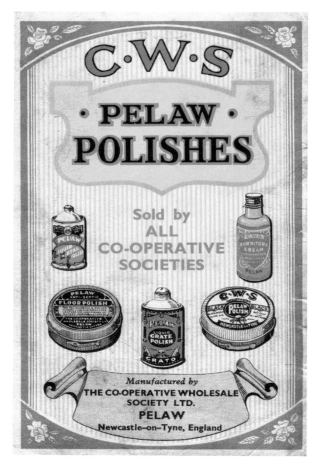

Delivery vans of the Blaydon Co-operative Society in front of the delivery department garages c1935.

Left: Advert for Pelaw Polishes c1912. Many areas in the North East had their own 'Co-op' stores and Co-operative Wholesale Society products, being both reasonably priced and good quality, could be found in every home.

The Co-op in Newgate Street in 1947, which offered Geordies a chance to see the world through their Travel Agency.

How about a sack of nutty slack? Delivery lorry of P G Walton Ltd coal dealer, 1943. With many homes still reliant on coal fired heating and cooking ranges, every house had its 'coal hole' and 'the coal man' was a regular sight on the streets of Newcastle up to the 1960s.

Sailor Salmon Slice and Sailor Savouries, two of the numerous canned fish products produced by Angus Watson 'The Sardine King' who created thousands of new jobs for local people at his City Road canneries during the hard times of the 1920s

The Ringtons Tea salesman on his rounds, 1956. Founded in Newcastle in 1907 by Samuel Smith, who opened his purpose-built factory and six-storey head office on Algernon Road in 1926. Inset: Advert for Ringtons Tea 'Free deliveries to all parts by own vans' 1937.

Minories Garages Ltd, petrol pumps and car showroom on Gallowgate 1956. Many of the popular cars and commercial vehicles of the day were on offer here such as Sunbeam-Talbot, Hillman, Humber and Commer, and all of them were British manufactured.

Advert for Newcastle Brown Ale 1942. The Blue Star trade mark was introduced in 1928, each of the five points of the star represented one of the five breweries that combined to form Newcastle Breweries. The illuminated blue star of the brewery that used to shine out from the city skyline was just as much a symbol of Newcastle as the Tyne Bridge itself.

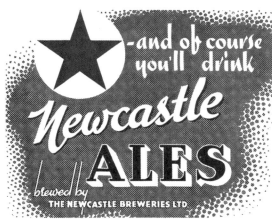

You'll enjoy the sport -

-and of course you'll drink

Newcastle ALES

brewed by THE NEWCASTLE BREWERIES LTD.

Above: Four of the Newcastle Breweries Commer diesel delivery vans 1959. Newcastle Brown Ale was launched in 1927 and, despite sales being confined to the North East when this photograph was taken, in excess of 300 million bottles of Newcastle Brown Ale had been sold.

Carrick's head office bakery staff, Cowgate, 1936. Carrick's had over 100 waitress service cafes and bakery shops across the North East. They were the sort of shops that everybody remembers with affection.

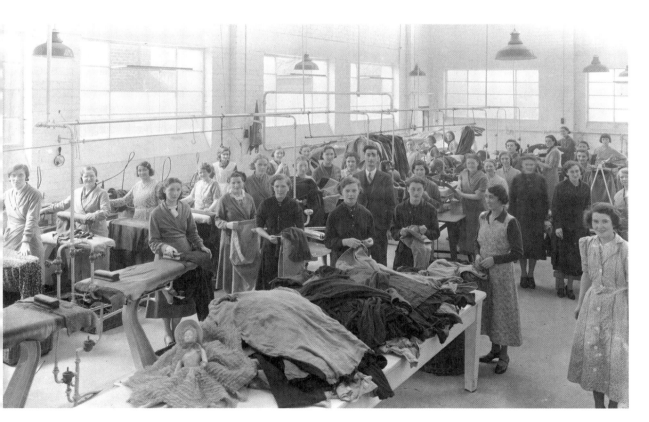

Hand ironing and pressing room at the Bradburn Dye Works, Heaton 1938. Newcastle had many factories making a host of products for both industrial and domestic markets. Much of the work was carried out on hands on production lines by both men and women.

Packing room with boxes of Rubicon tobacco at John Sinclair Ltd, Bath Lane 1949.

The tobacco leaf preparation department at the John Sinclair Ltd factory on Bath Lane 1949. Inset: Advert for Barneys tobacco made by John Sinclair Ltd, Newcastle, famous throughout the armed forces during the Second World War.

Packing room for the Metal Box Company factory at Heaton Junction, manufacturers of 'Flit' spray cans, 1956.

The Hadrian self-service grocery shop, Wallsend 1954. Opened with the message - 'It's on the shelf – Serve Yourself,' the concept of a self service shop was still new to the British public who were used to asking at a counter and being served with goods they wished to purchase.

Miss Doris Wright on the till of a slide-along check-out at a branch of Laws Stores 1956. Laws' supermarket chain had branches in many towns in the North East between 1907 and the 1980s.

Staff from J W Hindson & Sons printers 'roll out the barrel' on their works outing 1942. Cheers!

Staff ready for a works outing from A S Wilkin Ltd, Cremona Park Confectionery Works at Heaton, 1938.

Engineering firm C. A. Parsons and Company was one of the largest employers on Tyneside and here are some of workers enjoying a well earned break in the works canteen in 1923.

Chapter Five

SPORT

The crowd leaving St James' Park after the match c1910. A-state-of-the-art ground for its day, it had a capacity for crowds of up to 60,000.

The Newcastle United Football Team, season 1914-15. Geordie Newcastle is synonymous with football in good times and bad. This photograph sees the team at the end of its first glory era, crowned by winning the FA Cup in 1910 and abruptly ended by the outbreak of war in 1914.

Newcastle United F.C.

1914.   1915.

Right: Official programme for the 'local derby' match between Newcastle United and Sunderland on 23 March 1951. These were the days when 'Wor Jackie', the legendary Jackie Milburn NUFC's highest goal scorer, was playing and he scored the two goals for the team that won the FA Cup final against Blackpool in April 1951. Above: A crowd gathers in Newcastle to see the triumphant 'Toon' return with the cup.

St James Cycling Club in Newcastle c1930.

Mixed doubles in Benton. In the 1930s tennis was becoming more popular in the suburbs. Right: A walking race in 1912 drew the crowds.

Women football players in the North East c1918. During the First World War women's football teams became a phenomenon. Teams were permitted to join the FA and because so many of the players were engaged in munitions work they competed for what became known as 'The Munitionettes Cup.'

Swimmers prepare to take the plunge at Northumberland Road Baths in 1929

Bainbridge Memorial Church Amateur Football Club 1908-9. In the days before television both professional and amateur local football clubs would be followed as avidly as the Premier League is today and there were a number of local cups and shields that were fiercely contested.

Studio photograph of a Geordie husband and wife c1912. Sportsmen would often receive a silver fob as a prize or as a memento of the cup they had won and men of the North would often be seen proudly wearing a number of such fobs on their watch chain as a display of their prowess.

Nº 133

NEWCASTLE SPEEDWAY
BROUGH PARK

6d

OFFICIAL PROGRAMME

MONDAY, APRIL 16th, 1951.

MEETING NO. 5,

Newcastle v. White City (Glasgow)

KEMSLEY NORTHERN SHIELD.

Newcastle Speedway programme 1951. The opening meeting of Brough Park Speedway took place on 17 May 1929. The stadium became known as 'the jewel of the North', home to the 'Diamonds' and the 'Gems' racing teams.

Mixed Hockey team c1905. There was quite a vogue for hockey in the early 20th century and it was one of the few sports where there were mixed teams of men and women. North East teams stuck it out longer than many but at that time it was somewhat frowned upon by sport officialdom.

Armstrong College ladies hockey team 1913-14. One girl would recall with a wry smile that they had to maintain a demeanour befitting well bred young ladies, however 'on the field of play, armed with our sticks in our hands, we were demons!'

Start of two-mile harrier team race for the Co-operative Cup at the North East Coast Exhibition in 1929.

Prize winning cart advertising Greyhound Racing at Newcastle Stadium (Brough Park) 'Ye Mecca of Greyhound Racing in the North' c1938.

Boy gymnasts demonstrate strength, agility and balance at the Pageant of Youth held at Exhibition Stadium in 1929.

Highland Games competitors and Scottish country dancers at the Exhibition Stadium at the North East Coast Exhibition, 1929.

Chapter Six

ENTERTAINMENT

Smartly turned out carriages, drivers and passengers outside Eldon Place c1890

It is hardly surprising that many of the good times and events of Geordieland in the past had songs written about them, which were sold as cheap song sheets at the events themselves be they high days or hangings. Others, often far better than the doggerel of the broadsides, were written and sung by local music hall artists. Probably the most enduring and above all catchy song is 'Blaydon Races' originally written and performed by local songwriter and entertainer George 'Geordie' Ridley in 1862. It tells the story of the journey to the Blaydon Races, horse races first staged (officially at least) on Blaydon Island in 1861. Opposite: There are very slightly different versions of the exact words, here is the version written in Great Grandad's song book from the 1890s.

The Blaydon Races

Aa went to Blaydon Races, 'twas on the ninth of Joon,
Eiteen hundred an' sixty-two, on a summer's efternoon;
Aa tyuk the 'bus frae Balmbra's, an' she wis heavy laden,
Away we went alang Collingwood Street, that's on the road to Blaydon.

Chorus:
Ah me lads, ye shudda seen us gannin',
Passin' the foaks alang the road just as they wor stannin';
Thor wes lots o' lads an' lassies there, all wi' smiling faces,
Gannin' alang the Scotswood Road, to see the Blaydon Races.

We flew past Airmstrong's factory, and up to the "Robin Adair",
Just gannin' doon te the railway bridge, the bus wheel flew off there.
The lassies lost their crinolines off, an' the veils that hide their faces,
An' aw got two black eyes an' a broken nose gannin' te Blaydon Races.

(chorus)

When we gat the wheel put on away we went agyen,
But them that had their noses broke they cam back ower hyem;
Sum went to the Dispensary an' uthers to Doctor Gibbs,
An' sum to the Infirmary, to mend their broken ribs.

(chorus)

Noo when we gat to Paradise thor wes bonny gam begun.
Thor was fower and twenty on the 'bus, man, hoo they danced an' sung;
They called on me to sing a sang, aa sung them 'Paddy Fagan',
Aa danced a jig an' swung me twig that day aa went to Blaydon.

(chorus)

We flew across the Chain Bridge reet into Blaydon toon,
The bellman he was callin' there, they call him Jacky Broon;
Aa saw him talkin' to sum cheps, an' them he was pursuadin'
To gan an' see Geordy Ridley's concert in the Mechanic's Hall at Blaydon.

(chorus)

The rain it poor'd aall the day an' myed the groond quite muddy,
Coffy Johnny had a white hat on – they wor shootin' "Whe stole the cuddy."
There wes spice stalls an' munkey shows an' aud wives selling ciders,
An' a chep wiv a hapenny roond aboot, shootin' "Noo, me lads, for riders."

Paramount Theatre (later the Odeon) on Pilgrim Street, in 1938. The old theatre recently became the latest in a long line of Newcastle cinemas to be demolished. Inset: The auditorium of the Paramount in 1931. Decorated in superb deco style, equipped with one of the largest Wurlitzer organs in the North, it was capable of seating houses of 2,604.

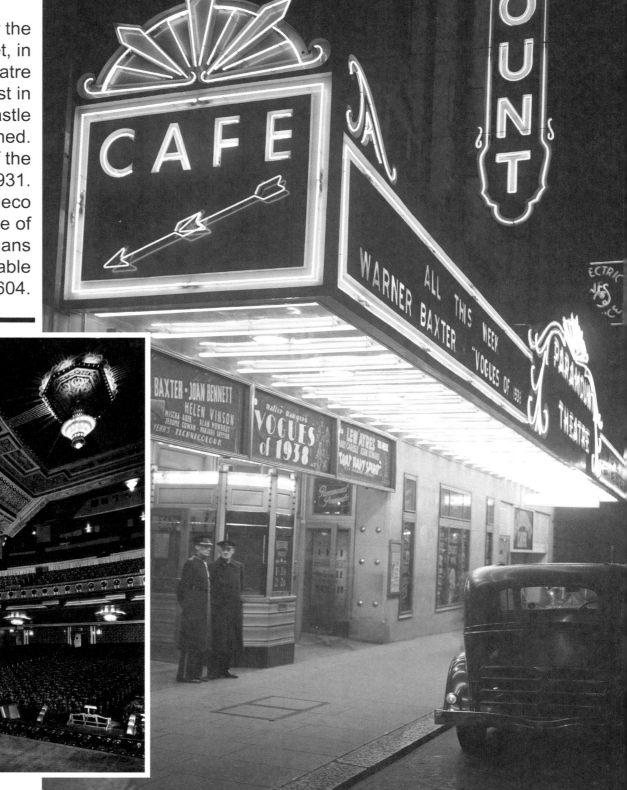

The New Westgate cinema in 1933 was for a time the largest in the city. Decorated in Italian Renaissance style it would draw in film lovers with large posters for upcoming films such as the one pictured above for 'The Thin Man' in 1934.

Roller skating at Exhibition Hall, St Mary's Place, Newcastle c1908. There were sessions in the morning, afternoon and evening, all accompanied by a military band. Smartly uniformed tutors were on hand and skates could be hired for 1 shilling.

Hundreds of Newcastle folk enjoying the band playing in the bandstand at Leazes Park c1912. Parks were very popular places to gather at weekends for walks among well tended and colourful gardens, meet and make friends, have picnics and enjoy live music.

A Geordie girls' day out to one of the most popular local beauty spots at Jesmond Dene c1911.

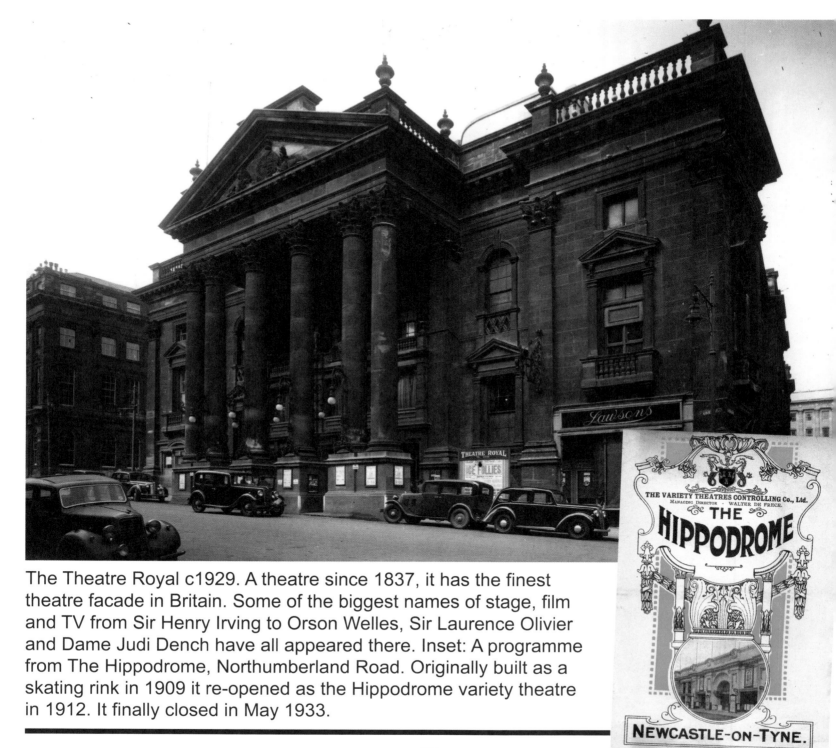

The Theatre Royal c1929. A theatre since 1837, it has the finest theatre facade in Britain. Some of the biggest names of stage, film and TV from Sir Henry Irving to Orson Welles, Sir Laurence Olivier and Dame Judi Dench have all appeared there. Inset: A programme from The Hippodrome, Northumberland Road. Originally built as a skating rink in 1909 it re-opened as the Hippodrome variety theatre in 1912. It finally closed in May 1933.

LILY MORRIS. (ALADDIN)

PHOTO. STUART & WINFIELD.   G.HASTINGS. N/C.93.

NEIL KENYON. (WIDOW TWANKEY)(HA HA)

PHOTO. STUART & WINFIELD.   G.HASTINGS N/C.97.

Geordie audiences have always enjoyed pantomime. This is Lily Morris as Aladdin and Neil Kenyon as Widow Twankey at The Theatre Royal in 1907.

NEWCASTLE EMPIRE

Price 3D.

PROGRAMME

TENNANT

Left: A 1948 programme for Newcastle Empire Theatre that stood on Newgate Street. Laurel and Hardy, Ivor Novello, and even Des O'Conner performed there over the years but it closed in the 1960s and was demolished in 1963.

Bessie Featherstone was Aladdin in the Tyne Theatre for their 1906-7 pantomime. Back by popular demand she gave her all on stage but had been suffering from typhoid fever and died in her apartment on 1 January 1907.

A Geordie amateur theatrical group March 1944. For generations am dram has been the start of many careers in the acting profession for the talented on Tyneside.

One of the highlights of the public entertainments for Geordie Newcastle is The Hoppings, usually held on Town Moor. However, when war broke out in August 1914 the Moor was being used for military encampments and training and the Hoppings had to be moved. This photograph shows when it was held at Greenwater Pool, Jesmond Vale in that year.

The African Jungle Circus at the Hoppings c1935.

Motorcycle and motor car stunt riders ready to ride on a perpendicular wall at the Hoppings c1935.

Dodgem cars at the Hoppings c1935.

On the mat at the bottom of the Helter Skelter at the Hoppings c1935.

A cheeky smile from from one of the carriages on the train carousel at the Hoppings c1935.

Chapter Seven

DAYS TO REMEMBER

Unveiling of the Joseph Cowan statue on Westgate Road, 7 July 1906. Cowan was a radical Liberal politician and a popular MP for Newcastle who did much for the people and culture of the city. He was firm in his views and his family business was brickmaking, thus he was known as 'The Blaydon Brick.'

UNVEILING NORTHUMBERLAND WAR MEMORIAL JUNE 22ᴺᴰ 1908. C.H Nₑ

The unveiling of the 24m high memorial on the Haymarket, unveiled by Lieutenant General Sir Laurence Oliphant on 22 June 1908 to commemorate the 370 soldiers of Northumbrian regiments that fell in the South African War (1899-1902). Note the lower figure holds a long palm frond, which is now missing from the memorial.

Some of the first aeroplanes to fly over Newcastle were part of the circuit of Britain aviation race for a prize of £10,000 in July 1911. The planes needed to refuel regularly and be checked over for faults. The Gosforth Park aerodrome provided one of the landing grounds and tens of thousands turned out to catch a glimpse of the aircraft in the air or on the field.

Members of the Newcastle Branch of the National Union of Women's Suffrage Societies, (they were Suffragists, rather than Suffragettes) who argued for the vote by peaceful, legal means, photographed on Northumberland Street c1910. A number of them joined 'The Great Pilgrimage' march on the Great North Route from Newcastle to London in 1913.

The Drums of 16th (Service) Battalion, The Northumberland Fusiliers, 'The Newcastle Commercials' 1915. Newcastle raised more battalions of volunteer soldiers for 'Kitchener's Army' than any other city outside London.

Newcastle also raised two battalions of 'Tyneside Pioneers' who became 18th and 19th (Service) Battalions, Northumberland Fusiliers.

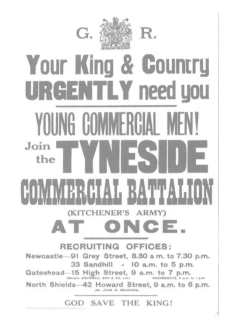

G. R.

Your King & Country URGENTLY need you

YOUNG COMMERCIAL MEN!

Join the **TYNESIDE COMMERCIAL BATTALION**

(KITCHENER'S ARMY)

AT ONCE.

RECRUITING OFFICES:
Newcastle—91 Grey Street, 8.30 a.m. to 7.30 p.m.
33 Sandhill - 10 a.m. to 5 p.m.
Gateshead—15 High Street, 9 a.m. to 7 p.m.
(Messrs. SNOWBALL SON & CO. Ltd.) WEDNESDAYS, 9 a.m. to 1 p.m.
North Shields—42 Howard Street, 9 a.m. to 6 p.m.
(Mr. JOHN W. MEADOWS.)

GOD SAVE THE KING!

Recruitment poster for the 'Newcastle Commercials,' 1914. Left: A postcard showing some of the roles Newcastle women performed during the First World War. From munitions to tram clippies, postwomen to women's branches of the three services, Geordie lasses did their bit!

BRITAIN'S WAR WORKERS

BEHOLD THE SMART POST LADY
WHO BRINGS LETTERS TO OUR HOUSES.
ALSO THE TRAM CONDUCTOR
AND THESE SWEET THINGS IN TROUSERS.

Pipers of 1st Battalion, Tyneside Scottish 1915. Newcastle raised a Brigade of four battalions of Tyneside Scottish soldiers. Many were not actually Scottish, but joined so they could serve with their pals and for the crack of wearing a kilt. Sadly the War Office would only permit the pipers to wear the kilt but all ranks were granted Scottish head dress. Right, recruiting poster for the Tyneside Scottish produced by Andrew Reid & Co, that published their famous motto 'Harder Than Hammers' for the first time, 1914.

"SCOTLAND FOR EVER."

TYNESIDE SCOTTISH BRIGADE
"Harder than Hammers"

SCOTSMEN ON TYNESIDE

are given the opportunity to
defend their Country's honour by

ENROLLING NOW

in this fine Brigade which is quickly being
filled with the Toughest, Hardest and
Best Tyneside Fighting Men.

AGE LIMIT 19 TO 45
HEIGHT, 5ft. 3ins. CHEST, 34ins.

Central Recruiting Office:
9 Grainger Street West, Newcastle
BRANCHES IN MOST TYNESIDE TOWNS

ONE MAN TO-DAY WORTH THREE IN THREE MONTHS.
GOD SAVE THE KING.

Andrew Reid & Company, Limited.

Below: Recruiting poster to raise a battalion of Tyneside Irish, 1914. They too raised a Brigade of four Battalions.

The Duke of Northumberland handing the Colour of the Tyneside Irish to Hon. Colonel Sir Johnstone Wallace, to the left of them are Colour Parties of the Tyneside Scottish, at a special service on the Town Moor 1919. The Newcastle Commercials, Tyneside Scottish and Tyneside Irish all 'went over the top' on the first day of the Battle of the Somme on 1 July 1916 and suffered terrible casualties. The Northumberland Fusiliers lost more men on that fateful day than any other regiment.

THE CALL TO ARMS!
YOUR COUNTRY NEEDS YOU!
JOIN THE
TYNESIDE
IRISH BATTALION

All eligible Irishmen are cordially invited to join at once to fight for the great principles of freedom and the rights of small nations, and against military tyranny and despotism.

Proposal Forms are obtainable in all districts in Northumberland and Durham, or from the
CENTRAL RECRUITING OFFICE, Town Hall,
Corn Exchange,
Newcastle-on-Tyne.
JOHN MULCAHY
GERALD STONEY Joint Secs.

GOD SAVE OUR KING AND COUNTRY!

The Response, one of the finest war memorials in the country, commemorates B Company 9th Battalion, 16th (Newcastle Commercials) 18th and 19th Battalion (1st and 2nd Tyneside Pioneers) Northumberland Fusiliers raised by the Newcastle & Gateshead Chamber of Commerce in 1914. Funded by local businessman Sir George Renwick in thanks for the safe return for all five of his sons, this unique monument was unveiled by HRH The Prince of Wales on 5 July 1923.

Some of the First World War veterans who paraded on the occasion of the visit of the Prince of Wales to Newcastle in 1923. Some had lost limbs, others could only walk aided by sticks but they marched with Geordie pride.

OPENING OF THE TYNE BRIDGE, 10th, OCTOBER 1928, by His Majesty The King.

Crowds line the route to wave at the King George V and Queen Mary as they rode through the streets in an open carriage when they came to open the Tyne Bridge on 10 October 1928.

Testing exercises on what would be opened as the King Edward VII Bridge in 1906

The Festival Hall and Fountain at the North East Coast Exhibition, 1929. It was billed as a world's fair showcase of engineering skills, industries, trade and arts of Newcastle and the north east.

FESTIVAL HALL AND FOUNTAIN.
NORTH EAST COAST EXHIBITION, 1929,
NEWCASTLE-UPON-TYNE

PALACE OF INDUSTRIES.
NORTH EAST COAST EXHIBITION, 1929,
NEWCASTLE-UPON-TYNE

The Palace of Industries at the North-East Coast Exhibition. Staged on Exhibition Park between May-October 1929 it was attended by an average of 30,000 visitors a day. The only building left today is the Rotunda to the right of the picture.

NEWCASTLE-ON-TYNE HISTORICAL PAGEANT. Photo.
P. 12. THE EMPEROR HADRIAN COMMANDS THE BUILDING OF THE Newc
ROMAN BRIDGE AT NEWCASTLE, A.D.122. QUEEN AMELDUNA SALUTING.

Following on the success of the North East Coast Exhibition the Newcastle Upon Tyne Historical Pageant was staged on Leazes Park in 1931. Spectators were treated to dramatic episodes of regional history from Roman Emperor Hadrian commanding the building of the bridge to an eighteenth century fair.

The Townswomen's Guild also celebrated the 1937 Coronation with an all nations pageant.

Programme for the events in Newcastle to celebrate the Coronation of their Majesties King George VI and Queen Elizabeth – and of course every child was also given a coronation mug as a souvenir too.

Wharrier Street Air Raid Precautions Ambulance Section, 1941. When war came again Newcastle suffered numerous air raids and it was volunteer ambulance crews of trained men and women like this one who responded to the calls for help.

Trained and armed to defend the Toon - F Company (Newcastle East), 12th Battalion, Northumberland Home Guard.

The Overseas League organised Empire Days before and during the war to raise money for comforts for troops serving abroad (mostly cigarettes). Children would donate a penny and receive a thank-you certificate and as ever Geordie folks generously supported charities throughout the war.

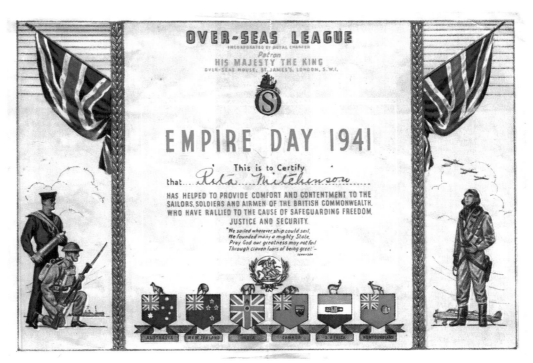

OVER-SEAS LEAGUE
INCORPORATED BY ROYAL CHARTER
Patron
HIS MAJESTY THE KING
OVER-SEAS HOUSE, ST.JAMES'S. LONDON, S.W.I.

EMPIRE DAY 1941

This is to Certify
that Rita Mitchenson
HAS HELPED TO PROVIDE COMFORT AND CONTENTMENT TO THE
SAILORS, SOLDIERS AND AIRMEN OF THE BRITISH COMMONWEALTH,
WHO HAVE RALLIED TO THE CAUSE OF SAFEGUARDING FREEDOM,
JUSTICE AND SECURITY.

"We sailed wherever ship could sail,
We founded many a mighty State,
Pray God our greatness may not fail
Through craven fears of being great!" -
TENNYSON

The Tyne (North Sector) Home Guard Military band on the Newcastle Victory Parade, 8 June 1946

Neil R. Storey is an award winning social historian who guest lectures all over the UK. He has published over forty books and has produced countless articles for national magazines and journals. He has a nationally respected archive of social and military history photographs and ephemera and regularly appears as guest expert on television and radio factual programmes and documentaries including BBC's Who Do You Think You Are?.

Fiona Kay is a born and bred Geordie girl and proud of it. She works extensively in archives and has a remarkable collection of North East social history and fashion photographs to illustrate her books and talks.

They are both creative consultants for national and local history projects that make history interactive and accessible for all ages .

Neil and Fiona formed their dynamic writing partnership in 2016, their books include: *Newcastle Battalions on the Somme* (Tyne Bridge 2016), *Voices of the First World War: Northumberland & Tyneside's War* (Amberley 2017), *Women in the Second World War* (Amberley 2019) and *Newcastle and Tyneside in the Second World War* (Tyne Bridge 2020)